PROCEEDINGS OF A MEETING,

AND

REPORT

OF A

COMMITTEE OF THE CITIZENS,

OF CLEVELAND,

IN RELATION TO

STEAMBOAT DISASTERS

ON THE WESTERN LAKES.

PUBLISHED BY THE COMMITTEE, CLEVELAND, 1850.

CLEVELAND;
STEAM PRESS OF HARRIS, FAIRBANKS & CO.,
Herard Job Office, Merchants Exchange.

1850.

INTRODUCTORY.

The proceedings embodied in the following pages it will be noticed, were more immediately prompted by the burning of the steamer G. P. Griffith, and the almost unprecedented destruction of life attending that disaster.

Public attention had, however, been directed for some years to the reckless risk of life evinced by many of the proprietors of steamboats on Western waters, who, induced by cupidity or through carelessness, and in defiance of existing laws, put afloat boats illy built and unprovided with the means of saving life, in case of accident, or which had been long rendered unseaworthy by age and decay.

The wreck of the Chesapeake by collision, three years since, and the loss of eight lives, was the first to cause a general expression of the prevailing sentiment upon the subject. The feeling was increased by other disasters, attributable to want of care, until this season, a rapid succession of collisions, conflagrations, and explosions, have called forth a unanimous voice in condemnation of this reckless and wanton destruction of life and property, and loudly demands that Congress should take prompt, energetic, and *effectual* means to put a stop to it, and protect the public. Within the last five months alone there have been no less than three explosions—the collision of two steamboats and one total destruction by fire—resulting in the loss of 376 lives; also, several very dangerous collisions and many fires on Boats, where fortunately no lives were lost. Even while this is being penned, "Extras" are in rapid circulation, announcing the explosion of the AMERICA, attended by a great loss of life, this day.

The G. P. Griffith was considered one of the better class of Boats—about 560 tons burden. She was owned seven-eighths by Capt. C. C. Roby, and those he represented, and one-eighth by the 1st Engineer, D. R. Stebbins. She left Buffalo on Sunday, June 16, 1850, at 10 A. M., for Toledo, with a large load of passengers, numbering, it is supposed, over 300. The Boat was first discovered to be on fire at half past 3 o'clock, A. M., of the 17th, about 15 miles below Cleveland, and while she was about 1½ mile from shore. The fire hose, which was constantly attached, had only to be unreeled, and immediately a stream of water was directed into the freight hold, which was completely filled with flame, but it was of no avail. In five minutes, the Boat was headed towards shore, and in ten minutes afterwards, she struck in 9 feet water, about 50 rods from the beach. She was instantly enveloped in flame, and the passengers, who had principally huddled forward and at the gang ways, with one shriek of despair, went overboard, sinking even where they struck, and in their death struggle grappling each other so that groups of from 3 to 8 bodies were recovered firmly locked together, and with difficulty separated from their icy embrace. The Captain, with his wife, mother, two daughters and sister-in-law—all perished together—only 31 escaped—among whom were the Engineer and first and second Mates.

This is the more astonishing, as the Lake was perfectly calm, the water not chilly, and the distance to wading depth not more than 40 rods.

Not a boat was launched, nor even a door wrenched from its hinges and thrown overboard, a few sticks of wood and the gang-way plank were shoved over, but not one was saved by them. In twenty minutes from the first alarm, the tragedy was over, and about 275, out of a little over 300 passengers and crew, had perished. 223 bodies have been recovered, of which 106 were buried in trenches in the bank of the Lake overlooking the scene of their death—the remainder were taken to Cleveland or Willoughby or sent to their former homes.

LAKE STEAMBOAT DISASTERS.

At a Public Meeting, held at Empire Hall, on Monday evening, July 1st, 1850, His Honor the Mayor, WM. CASE, was called to the Chair, and WM. MILFORD, appointed Secretary.

The Chairman having stated the object of the meeting, Samuel Starkweather, Esq., arose, and in a thrilling and soul-stirring speech, reviewed the late melancholy occurrence of the burning of the Steamer Griffith, and urged in a powerful and effective manner the duty of the citizens of Cleveland in view of the distressing event.

H. B. Payne, Samuel Williamson, and Samuel Starkweather, Esqrs., were appointed a committee to draft and submit resolutions.

During the absence of the committee, J. L. Weatherly, Esq., addressed the meeting, and explained in a lucid and satisfactory manner, the probable cause of the burning of the Griffith, namely, that *the fire originated in the fire hold in consequence of defect in the water jacket.*

Mr. Payne, from the committee on resolutions, submitted the following, which were read and unanimously adopted :

Whereas, The burning of the Steamboat G. P. Griffith, on the morning of the 17th of June, in the vicinity of this city, occasioned the sudden death of more than 300 human beings, and constitutes a frightful and appalling disaster, unparalleled in the history of Lake Navigation :

And *Whereas*, its dreadful fatality is calculated to enlist public sympathy in behalf of surviving relatives and friends, as well as the circumstances under which it happened—in such close proximity to the shore—in the day time—and with such slight means of escape from the wreck—demand a more thorough scrutiny into the securities which are and should be provided for the preservation of life on board of Steamboats engaged in the carriage of passengers: And *Whereas*, the people of Cleveland, from their vicinity to the scene of disaster, their intercourse with the surviving passengers, and from personal observation, are enabled to judge intelligibly of the cause and consequences of this sad event, therefore,

Resolved, That to the surviving relatives, whether in this country or in Europe, who, by this inscrutable dispensation of Providence, have been thus severely bereaved of their associates and friends, we tender our sincere and earnest sympathies, while we assure them that every possible effort has been made to secure to the deceased the honors of a christian burial.

Resolved, That the citizens of Willoughby, together with the authorities and public spirited individuals of this city, and others who co-operated with them, are richly entitled to the warm thanks of this meeting and of good men everywhere, for their prompt and hazardous exertions in rescuing the surviving passengers from the wreck; and especially for their long-continued, unwearied and successful efforts to recover the dead, and provide for their interment.

Resolved, That although we are unable to designate the precise part of the boat where the fire originated, yet we have no hesitancy in declaring it as our opinion that the Griffith was not constructed with sufficient securities against danger from fire, and was not furnished with suitable means for enabling passengers to escape from the flames. And further, it is our opinion that the inspection, provided by the law of Congress, has been inefficiently executed, and that the law itself is radically defective.

Resolved, As the deliberate judgment of this meeting, that every steamboat should be prohibited by law from carrying passengers, until it has been thoroughly inspected by a competent Inspector, appointed under the authority of the Executive, and whose compensation should be made entirely independent of steamboat proprietors: and whenever practicable, such inspections should begin with the construction of the boat. And that new and additional safeguards around the boilers and pipes—an approved apparatus for extinguishing fire—and a full complement of planks and life preservers should be regarded as equally indispensable with the usual seaworthiness of the hull or the good order and condition of the engine.

Resolved, That until such a law shall be enacted and carried into execution, we recommend to the proprietors of Steamboats on the Lakes, to cause their boats to be thoroughly overhauled and examined, and forthwith furnished with fire apparatus, planks and life preservers, as specified in the foregoing resolutions, and that the names of all boats complying with that recommendation be published for the information of the public.

J. G. M'Curdy, Esq., submitted the following, which was adopted:

Resolved, That a committee of six be appointed by the Chair to obtain subscriptions to defray the expense of the purchase and enclosure of the ground for the interment of the bodies recovered from the Lake, of passengers lost from the late Steamer Griffith, and other incidental expenses for that object, which cannot appropriately be provided for by the City Council or the Township of Willoughby.

The following gentlemen were appointed a committee to collect funds to defray the expenses incurred in taking charge of, and burying the dead bodies recovered from the wreck of the Griffith, and to purchase and enclose the burial ground:

Messrs. J. G. Stockley, B. Rouse, A. Seywert, G. Lott, and Thiele Herbert.

A committee of 16 were appointed to act in conjunction with a committee to be appointed by the Council to draft a Memorial to Congress and an Address to the People. Said committee composed of the following gentlemen:

Messrs. J. L. Weatherly, Samuel Starkweather, E. T. Sterling, J. A. Harris, J. C. Vaughan, J W. Gray, N. C. Winslow, C. Bradburn, J. Gillett, L. Rawson, A. H. Barney, E. Hessenmueller, L. M. Hubby, J. Lyman, Wm. Milford, Benj. A. Standart.

The committee appointed by the City Council was composed as follows:

The Mayor, A Seymour, A. Hughes, S. Williamson, John Gill.

WILLIAM CASE, *Chairman*.

WM. MILFORD, *Secretary*.

MEETING OF THE COMMITTEE.

The Committee appointed by the citizens of Cleveland to consider the causes of Steamboat Disasters and the means of prevention, met July 16th, at the Council Chamber, J. L. Weatherly Chairman. When the Committee was organized, the following report prepared by him was read:

REPORT

Of the Cleveland Committee on Steam Navigation on the Western Lakes.

The destruction of the Steamboat G. P. Griffith, by fire, on Lake Erie, on the 17th June, 1850, with the loss of about 275 lives, induced the citizens of Cleveland to hold a Public Meeting on the subject of Steam Vessel disasters on the Lakes, and a Committee was appointed to report, if practicable, the number of disasters on the Lakes by fires, explosions, and collisions, and what further Congressional Legislation is necessary to enforce greater care in the navigation of steam vessels, that life and property may be more secure.

The Committee are aware of the importance of the task assigned them, and of the total impossibility of recommending such measures for the avoidance of disasters as will meet with universal favor, but, having given the subject a careful investigation, and many of them having the experience of several years observation, they hope to make some suggestions of practical benefit that may induce others of greater experience to add more useful advice. All familiar with the navigation of the Lakes, willingly concede that the present management of steam vessels is accompanied with great hazard of life and property, and that a constant feeling of insecurity and danger prevails with passengers on the Lakes. That this feeling does not arise from nervous timidity, but has a well-founded existence in actual danger, is, unfortunately, too well substantiated, in the great loss of life and property which has occurred within a few years. We do not purpose bringing before the public the lamentable disaster of the Griffith, for we can give no additional facts to those already furnished by the public press. It is one of a series of disasters which should long since have attracted more direct attention in the vicinity of the Lakes, and led to energetic measures for correcting the evil. The past cannot be redeemed ; but, as facts and figures connected with it are reliable data for estimating such hazards, we give the following statement of the loss of lives by fire, explosions and collisions, on the Western Lakes, within a few years. We do not assert that the loss of life in each disaster is entirely accurate, but it is as near so as the nature of such disasters will admit, and it is believed that in the aggregate they fall rather under than over the actual loss:

EXPLOSIONS.

Year	Months	Name of Steamer.	Place.	Lives Lost.	Total.
1830	Nov'r.	William Peacock	Lake Erie	15	
1835	......	Commodore Perry	Eake Erie	6	
1840	August	Erie	Lake Erie	6	
1844	June	General Vance	Detroit River	6	
1849	May	Louisiana	Lake Erie	4	
1850	March	Troy	Lake Erie	14	
1850	April	Anthony Wayne	Lake Erie	60	111

FIRES.

Year	Month.	Name of Steamer.	Place.	Lives Lost.	Total.
1836	......	W. F. P. Taylor	Lake Erie	1	
1838	Juue 2	Washington 2d	Lake Erie	55	
1839	Sep't.	Great Western	Detroit River		
1841	Aug. 9	Erie	Lake Erie	240	
1842	Nov.	Vermillion	Huron River	5	
1847	Nov. 20	Phœnix	Lake Mich'n.	200	
1848	June 24	Speed	Ottawa River		
1848	Sep. 20	Goliath	Lake Huron	18	
1849	July 31	Chicago	Buffalo Creek		
1849	Oct.	Waterloo	Niagara River		
1850	Jue 17	G. P. Griffith	Lake Erie	275	804

COLLISIONS BY STEAM.

Year	Month.	Name of Steamer.	Place.	Lives Lost.	Total.
1840	August	St. Erie sunk st. Minisetunk, ...	Det River		
----	------	St. Com. Perry with a sail vessel,	Lake Erie	1	
1845	Aug 12	St. London sunk st. Kent,.....	Lake Erie	13	
1846	June	St. Bunker Hill and brig Fashion,	--------		
----	------	badly injured,.............	Lake Erie		
1846	Nov 13	St. Red Jacket sunk st. St. Clair,	Det River		
1846	Nov 16	St. Wolcott sunk by contact with	--------		
----	------	brig L. A. Blossom,........	Det River		
1847	May	Pro. Genesee Chief sunk sch.	--------		
----	------	Cuba,..................	L. Ontario		
1847	June 8	St. Saratoga and pro. Lady of the	--------		
----	------	Lake,..................	Lake Erie		
1847	June 9	St. Constellation sunk scow Rough	--------		
----	------	and Ready...............	Lake Erie		
1847	June 9	St. Chesapeake and schr. J. F.	--------		
----	------	Porter, both sunk,.........	Lake Erie	8	
1847	June10	St. Bunker Hill and pro Princeton,	Lake Erie		
1847	June11	St. Oregon and brig Empire,...	L Huron		
1847	June16	Pro. Manhattan sunk Sch. Saltillo,	L StClair		
----	------	St. Louisiana ran into st. Romeo,.	L St Clair		
1847	June21	St. Detroit & brig S. F. Gale,..	L Mich'n.		
1847	June	St. Bunker Hill and st. Gen. Scott,	Lake Erie		
1847	Aug 23	St. Nile and st. Wisconsin,.....	L Huron		
1847	Sept.	Pro. Pocahontas and pro. Racine,	Lake Erie		
1847	Oct. 6	St. Oregon and pro. Phœnix,...	Lake Erie		
1841	Oct	St. Gen. Scott sunk...........	L St Clair		
1848	July 3	St. Oregon ran into sch. Cadet, ..	Lake Erie		
1848	Oct 3	St. Arrow and pro. Oneida,....	Lake Erie		
1848	Nov 1	Pro. Princeton sunk brig Empire,	L Huron		
1849	June10	St. Saratoga and st. H. Hudson,.	Lake Erie	2	
1849	Aug 1	St. Troy sunk Sch'r. Acorn, ...	Lake Erie		
1849	Oct 17	St. Griffith sunk sch'r. California,	Lake Erie		
1849	Oct	St. Diamond ran into sch. Buena	--------		
----	------	Vista,..................	Lake Erie		
1849	Oct	St. Fashion ran into sch. Atlas,..	Lake Erie		
1850	May 7	St. Commerce sunk st. Dispatch,	Lake Erie	38	
1850	June 8	St. Louisiana ran into brig Gen'l.	--------		
----	June	Worth,..................	St Clair R		
1850		St. Keystone State sunk scow	--------		62
----		Comfort Ann,.............	Lake Erie		877

SUMMARY.

7	Explosions of Steam, killing	111
11	Fires,	804
31	Collisions,	62
	Total,	877

These figures tell too plainly the perils of Lake Navigation. Nearly 900 lives lost, nine-tenths of which are within nine years, and not one of them by casualties which could not have been averted by good judgment in the construction of the steamers, and proper care and watchfulness in their navigation. Shall such disasters continue without an effort to arrest them? Must travellers year after year traverse our Lakes with the dangers of a horrible death ever around them, and with no other feeling of security than the selfish hope of the provident that he may be saved by the means he has previously provided? Does not such recklessness involve the guilt of murder, and shall we make no effort to stay it?

The first query that suggests itself is, is the use of steam so connected with danger from fire, explosion and collision, that human ingenuity and prudent watchfulness cannot guard against them? We answer unhesitatingly no!—that skill and care can place it among the safest motive powers. The loss of life by fire so far exceeds the other casualties, that we turn our attention mainly to it, satisfied that in part of the auxiliary measures for guarding against it we reduce the liability to the other dangers. So far as we are aware, no serious fire has ever occurred on any steamer on the Lakes, originating in the cabins or other portions appropriated to passengers, but every such fire, with one exception, we believe, has originated under the main deck or in connection with the smoke pipes. If then the fire room and wood work adjacent to the smoke pipes are properly protected, the possibility of a fire is narrowed into a very small compass, which can be watched, and the fire extinguished with quite as much facility as if it occurred in a dwelling house or manufactory. Protection from fire to this extent, the travelling public have a right to demand, and when this is accomplished, the rest of the steamer (excepting the cargo hold) being in the occupancy and supervision of the passengers and the crew, a fire would be very early discovered, and with the usual means at hand, if in serviceable order, could be promptly extinguished. We anticipate no difficulty in protecting the "fire hold" from the danger of fire, if the following precautions are carefully carried into practice: Prohibit the placing of fuel of any kind in the fire hold—remove the bulk head so far from the front of the furnace as to avoid all danger of its ignition—protect the flooring in front of the furnace by metal, with water underneath it—have the furnace and boilers so constructed that there shall be at all times a body of water outside of the fire, and extending under the ash pan, and have the smoke chamber and pipes protected by a suitable water jacket extending above the hurricane deck a safe distance. With these arrangements, and connecting rods on the main deck, to let off a free head of steam from the boilers into the "fire hold," we believe there would be scarcely a possibility, under any circumstances, of a fire making any alarming progress in that portion of a vessel. The practicability of this construction no one will deny, and its expense can be the only objection. To this objection we reply, first, that the safety of human life and property demands a safe construction of the mode of conveyance when practicable. Second, that the expense can easily be met by the owners, by stripping the cabin of a portion of its extravagant furniture. Thousands of dollars are uselessly wasted in decorating the cabin, that adds nothing to the comfort of the passengers, and ministers only to the pride of ownership, because it can be displayed, and to the kindred vanity of the captain. Safety of life, with substantial conveniences and comfort to the traveller, should be the desideratum in the construction of steam vessels, and not lavish expenditures in decorations which merely amuse by their novelty and costliness for a few hours, but are too often, by their combustibility, an additional aid in the destruction of the passengers.

The means for the preservation of life after it is in danger are desirable, but all past experience has shown that boats, life preservers, planks and other expedients, are not in available places, after a few months passed without accident, and through the confusion and paralysis of the moment, are seldom used to any considerable extent.

Prevention is therefore the only reliable remedy, using other expedients as mere auxiliaries for safety.

In the record we have given of the loss of life, we have purposely omitted any notice of the numerous fires which have occurred on other steam vessels, but extinguished without serious disaster. Without asserting it as an authentic fact, we mention the prevalent belief on the Lakes, that there is scarcely a steamboat navigating the lakes West of Buffalo that has not been on fire one or more times. With so much danger surrounding this mode of travel, it becomes the duty of all seriously to reflect on the insecure condition of steam vessels, and adopt some practical and universal mode of construction which shall largely diminish, if it does not entirely remove, the danger.

Past experience has shewn us that the owners and constructors of steam vessels and their machinery will not voluntarily abandon the present defective mode of construction, and that coercion alone must force them into the proper precautions. Fortunately for public safety that power exists with Congress, and suitable laws passed by it and then enforced by United States officers, acting under it, can reach the evil. The law now in existence, passed July 7, 1838, entitled "An Act to provide for the better security of the lives of passengers on board of vessels propelled in whole or in part by steam," has many valuable provisions in it, but it is defective in several essentials, the leading ones of which, we conceive to be in the mode of appointing Inspectors of such vessels; their inadequate compensation; and in not providing suitable United States officers who shall investigate and prosecute offenders for infraction of the law. Whilst it imposes suitable penalties for its non-observance, it throws upon the public the burden of prosecuting the offender, offering to the complainant one half of the penalty on conviction. The stigma attached to a voluntary complainant receiving his reward, is so odious to the mass of our citizens, that every one revolts from the duty, and the law has, as a natural consequence, become a dead letter. That the defects of the present law may be readily perceptible, we give a brief synopsis of each section of it, excepting sections 12 and 13, which we copy entire.

Section 1st, Requires owners of steamboats to obtain a new enrolment on or before October 1st, 1838, and take out a new license.

Section 2nd, Makes it unlawful to engage in transportation without the new license, and without complying with the provisions of this Act. Penalty Five Hundred Dollars—one half of which goes to the informer—the vessel liable for the penalty, and may be seized and proceeded against summarily by way of libel in any District Court of the United States having jurisdiction of the offence.

Section 3rd, Requires any District Judge of the United States, within whose District any ports of entry or delivery may be on the rivers and lakes, &c., to appoint competent Inspectors to judge the safety of hull and machinery, &c., stipulating they shall not be interested at the time in the manufacture of steam engines, &c. The Inspector to take an oath to perform his duties faithfully, and requiring him to give duplicate certificates of inspection.

Section 4th, Requires the Inspectors of *Hulls* to give the owners or masters duplicate certificates, stating the age of the boat, and whether she is seaworthy—the Inspector to receive a compensation of Five Dollars from the owner or master.

Section 5th, Requires the Inspector of *Boilers* to give duplicate certificates of the age of boilers and their soundness—one of them to be given to the Collector when applying for a license—the Inspector to receive Five Dollars compensation.

Section 6th, *Hulls* to be inspected once in 12 months, and the *Boilers* once in 6 months, certificates of which shall be delivered to the Collector where the boat has been enrolled or licensed, and on failure, the license shall be forfeited, and the owners subject to the same penalty as if the boat had been run without a license—experienced and skilful Engineers to be appointed, or owners and masters shall be held responsible for damages to the property of any passenger on board, occasioned by an explosion of the boiler or derangement of the engine or machinery.

Section 7th, Safety valve to be opened when the vessel stops for any purpose whatever, so as to keep the steam down to running guage—Penalty $200.

Section 8th, Vessels on the lakes, not over 200 tons, to have two yawl boats, each capable of carrying 20 persons; exceeding 200 tons, three long boats or yawls —Penalty $300.

Section 9th, Requires Steamers on the Lakes and seas to have a Suction Hose and Fire Engine and Hose, under a penalty of $300.

Section 10th, Requires signal lights at night—Penalty $200.

Section 11th, Penalties are to be sued for and recovered in the name of the United States in the District or Circuit Court of such District or Circuit where the offence shall have been committed, or forfeiture incurred, or in which the owner or master may reside—one half the penalty to the informer, and one half to the United States.

Section 12th, And be it further enacted, That every Captain, Engineer, Pilot, or other person employed on board of any steamboat or vessel, propelled in whole or in part by steam, by whose misconduct, negligence, or inattention to his or their respective duties, the life or lives of any person or persons on board said vessel may be destroyed, shall be deemed guilty of manslaughter, and upon conviction thereof, before any Circuit Court in the United States, shall be sentenced to confinement at hard labor for a period not more than ten years.

Section 13th, And be it further enacted, That in all suits and actions against Proprietors of Steamboats for injuries arising to property or person from the bursting of the boiler of any steamboat, or the collapse of a flue or other injurious escape of steam, the fact of such bursting, collapse, or injurious escape of steam, shall be taken as full prima facie evidence sufficient to charge the defendant, or those in his employment, with negligence, until he shall shew that no negligence has been committed by him or those in his employment.

The defects of this law are very perceptible; and,

leaving it to other sections of the country to suggest such amendments as their own peculiar wants require, we would recommend the following amendments to the law, to be applied to the Lakes:

1st. That every Steam Vessel now in existence on the Lakes, or hereafter to be constructed, shall, after a day named, have the "fire hold" and its appurtenances constructed as safely as we have recommended in this Report.

2d. No Steam Vessel shall leave port or pursue her navigation on the Lakes, without having the hatches on her "freight hold" so secured as to prevent any fire being communicated from the deck. Any evasion or infraction of this section shall make the master and owners liable to a penalty of Five Hundred Dollars for each offence.

3rd. The President of the United States to appoint three Engineers for the inspecting of Boilers, having practical experience as Engineers in running steam vessels, who shall be a "Board of Inspectors" for the Western Lakes, with a District assigned to each, one of whom shall be stationed on Lake Ontario, one on Lake Erie, and one on Lake Michigan, each of whom shall receive annual Salaries adequate to command the requisite talent.—Make it their duty as a Board to examine at appointed times every applicant for the situation of Engineer and Assistant Engineer, and permit no person to be employed in such capacities without a certificate from the Board of his ability to discharge such duties. Any person assuming such duties without such certificate to be liable to twelve months' imprisonment, and the owners or master to a fine of Five Hundred Dollars. Make it the duty of the Inspector of the District, in which the vessel receives her license, to know that the Engineers have such certificates, and in case of any other persons being employed for such duties, to prosecute such persons and the owners or master. The Inspector of the District, in which any infraction of the law is committed, to be the prosecutor in the Courts named by the law, and to receive one-half of the penalty recovered.

4th. The "Inspector" of each District shall select a capable ship carpenter for inspecting the Hulls of vessels, and pay him one dollar per hundred tons for such inspection—a copy of such inspection to be made in a book, kept by the U. S. Inspector. Amend section 13th so as to embrace loss of life and property by fire and by collision.

It will be seen that these amendments to the law of 1838, provide Government Officers for the inspection of Boilers, Machinery and Hulls ; and, as the Inspectors receive their compensation from Government, their pecuniary interests are kept aloof from the interests of Steamboat Owners and Captains. As the Prosecutors of any evasion or infraction of the law, they will receive one-half of the Penalty for their additional labor, which it is believed will keep them vigilant in the performance of their duty.

In providing for the safe construction of the Fire Department of the Steam Vessel and capable Engineers for running it, we believe all is done that can be by legislation for the protection of lives and property by fire and explosion ; and, as the 12th section holds the Officers of the Boats guilty of manslaughter for loss of tlife by collision, as well as fire and explosions, we believe that if the United States Inspectors do their duty as prescribed by the law, traveling on the Lakes will be made as safe as any other mode of conveyance. The Committee recommend that this report be published by he newspapers in the several cities on the Lakes, and that petitions to Congress embodying these views be circulated for signatures in those cities, and sent to their Representatives in Congress.

J. L. WEATHERLY, *Chairman.*

Report unanimously adopted.

The following Resolutions were then passed:

Resolved, That S. STARKWEATHER, and J. L. WEATHERLY prepare a memorial to Congress, embodying, in brief, the spirit and principles of this Report.

Resolved, That W. CASE, A. HUGHES and A. SEYMOUR be a committee to contract for the printing of five hundred copies of the Report in pamphlet form, and when so printed, to forward one or more copies to each member of Congress, and to every city on the Lakes.

Resolved, That J. C. VAUGHN, W. MILFORD and E. HESSENMUELLER, be a Committee to forward the Report and Memorial to THOMAS CORWIN of the Senate, and J. R. GIDDINGS of the House, requesting them to present the latter, and press the subject matter of both, before Congress.

The Committee then adjourned. In obedience to the first resolution above, the sub-Committee have prepared the following

MEMORIAL

To the Senate and House of Representatives of the U. S.

The great loss of life and property this year on the Western Lakes having called public attention to the defective construction of steam vessels navigating these Lakes, the undersigned, residing in Cleveland, County of Cuyahoga, State of Ohio, respectfully petition for the following amendments, with suitable penalties to the law of July 7, 1838, entitled, " An Act to provide for the better security of the lives of passengers on board of vessels propelled in whole or in part by steam," believing them necessary for the protection of travelers on the Western Lakes:

1st. A safer construction of Steam Vessels now afloat or hereafter built, by having a water surface outside of the furnace, boilers, smoke pipes, under the ash-pan, and a metal flooring, with water under it, in front of the furnace.

2nd. Every Steam Vessel, on leaving any port, to have the hatches on her cargo hold, and so secured as to prevent any fire being commnicated from the deck.

3rd. Provide for the appointment, by the President of the United States, of three competent Engineers, receiving an adequate salary from Government, for the examination of furnaces, boilers, and other portions of the fire department of every Steam Vessel—divide the Lakes into three Districts, appointing one Inspector to each—constitute the three a Board for the examination of Engineers and Assistant Engineers, and permit no person to act in these capacities without the Board's certificate of ability for such duties—require each Inspector to prosecute all infractions of the law in his District—giving him one-half of the penalty.

4th. Require each Inspector to appoint a competent ship-carpenter for the examination of Hulls—the Government paying him an adequate compensation.

We respectfully solicit your attention to the "Report of the Cleveland Committee on Steam Navigation on the Western Lakes," which accompanies this Petition; and, believing that your wisdom will find adequate means to relieve travelers, on the Western Lakes, from their present perils, your petitioners, as in duty bound, will ever pray.

www.ingramcontent.com/pod-product-compliance
Lightning Source LLC
LaVergne TN
LVHW020634110826
845149LV00004B/1178

* 9 7 8 1 4 1 8 1 9 1 4 8 1 *